The Cry of Bosnia
A personal Diary of the Bosnian War

GW00692145

THE CRY OF BOSNIA

A personal Diary of the Bosnian War

Elvira Simić

Genie Quest Publishing

Front cover photograph by
Rikard Larma/The Associated Press Ltd
Back cover photograph by
Edin Suljic
Maps by Philip Ford Design & Illustration

First published in 1998 by
Genie Quest Publishing Ltd.,
The Business Village, Broomhill Road,
London, SW18 4JQ, England.

ISBN 1 902084 00 4

Printed and bound in Great Britain by
The Ipswich Book Company Ltd.

To my son.
May all children live in a world of peace.

CONTENTS

PUBLISHER'S NOTE

It is remarkable to come across an eyewitness account of human tragedy recorded as it is happening, conveying the uncertainty, fear and utter disbelief in man's cruel hatred that springs from conflict. At the same time as horror and revulsion grip the innocent witness, we are given a rare insight into the vulnerability of the victims of war. There is the grasping for the smallest thread of hope, the creaking of any door opening up to the outside world and the desperate seeking of a means to escape from the madness surrounding them.

The Cry of Bosnia, witten by a Muslim woman, gives such an eyewitness account. It is a touching portrayal of survival whilst trying to make sense of life. The basic story is written in the form of diary notes and letters adapted by her brother Edin Suljic and the publisher. Some of the names have been changed to protect the privacy of the persons mentioned. The story sends a clear message to the world, depicting the senseless killing of innocent victims, the destruction of whole villages, and the uprooting of a section of a community which has lived in relative peace with its neighbours for a long time. Why this sudden hatred and ethnic cleansing of Bosnian Muslims?

We are deeply grateful to Martin Bell for writing the foreword to this unique story. Mr Bell has worked on assignments in eighty countries and covered eleven wars during his thirty-four years with the BBC. He was awarded the OBE in 1992 and voted Royal Television Society Reporter of the Year in 1993 for the second time (previously in 1977). He is at present Independent Member of Parliament for Tatton.

Mr Bell first visited Sarajevo at the end of the first week of the Bosnian war in April 1992 and witnessed the forced mass evacuation of some 20,000 victims. In his own book, "In Harm's Way – Reflections of a War-Zone Thug", he writes: "I shall remember it for the rest of my life as the day that Bosnia died …"

Martin Bell himself became a victim of the violence in this conflict as he was dramatically wounded by shrapnel whilst reporting live to millions of British television viewers. Undeterred, he soon returned for duty in war-torn Bosnia after a spell in hospital. His in-depth knowledge of the Bosnian war gives the reader a privileged insight into this difficult conflict. He generously shares his sentiments.

At the beginning of the war in former Yugoslavia, in April 1992, there was widespread belief in Europe that the war would not last until the first winter. It could not possibly go on any longer than a few months. A war in Europe was unheard of. Surely it could not happen again. But it did happen and the conflict is still going on, over six years later.

Have our senses gone numb? Have we stopped listening to the cries for help from the people in Bosnia? Let us not forget them. Let us give them hope.

Marie Norlen-Smith
Publisher

FOREWORD

An instinct to fight is ingrained in the nature and history of man. Wars have always been with us and probably always will be. All that we can hope for is to pre-empt them when we can, and when we cannot to moderate their effects and seek to end them by agreement or even by force. The only option that we do not have is indifference.

Yet this was the option chosen in large measure by the Western democracies in 1992 when confronted by the challenge of the war in Bosnia. The violence and bloodshed which attended the break-up of the old Yugoslavia were the most graphic signals of a new world disorder, occasioned by the end of the Cold War.

Hopes of a new era of peace and co-operation scarcely lasted beyond the first few weeks. Global tensions were indeed reduced, but regional ones intensified.

I saw this at first hand when the Berlin Wall came down in November 1989. I was re-assigned from Washington to Berlin, to report the triumph of democracy in Eastern Europe. It seemed both an enviable and peaceful posting, but it was nothing of the kind. I found myself covering almost nothing but conflict – first the Gulf War, then the short war in Slovenia and the longer wars in Croatia and then in Bosnia. All these were the effects and symbols of a new world disorder. They were dealt with by the global and regional powers in strikingly different ways.

The West was as resolute in its response to aggression in Kuwait as it was irresolute in its response to aggression in Bosnia. But Kuwait, of course, had oil. What if Bosnia had had oil wells along with its cornfields?

These were large questions. And so it was that I came to believe, from a vantage point at times too close to be safe, that the conflict in Bosnia was the most consequential war of our time. It mattered then and it matters now that we understand its importance.

It was also an archetypally modern war – not in the sense that it featured bright shining new weapons, arcade game technology and the sort of missiles that can stop and turn left at traffic lights. It didn't. Its principal weapons – mortars, rifles and artillery – were barely distinguishable from those of the First World War. Some were actually the same. Its bleak and lethal landscapes belonged to the same age of trench warfare and its only technical innovations – for those sad souls who are interested in these things – were the rocket-propelled 500 pound aircraft bomb and sea-mines rolled downhill into villages.

It was a modern war, however, in a different sense. It combined the use of weapons of mass destruction with a total indifference as to whether the targets were military or civilian. The distinction was simply not made, because it was not perceived. Entire populations were targeted, and because civilians were less able to protect themselves than soldiers they suffered higher casualties. The Laws of Armed Conflict – the Geneva Conventions – were defied and violated every day for three and a half years.

The Bosnian War was also a modern war in a further sense, that it matched the means of mass destruction with the means of mass communication. We in the press not only observed its barbarities – not all of them, but a quite sufficient proportion – but projected them through the power of television into the living rooms of the world.

I was not a campaigning or crusading reporter. It was not my style. But it was only human to expect that the suffering of so many innocent people, shown with such urgency and immediacy at the time when it happened, would have the effect of forcing our Governments to take some effective action to put an end to it.

Yet for more than three years the Governments produced nothing – or nothing but empty resolutions, cosmetic half-measures and a UN Force with impressive numbers but an insufficient mandate.

I look back on my time in Bosnia with a sense of regret, and even of shame, that even the most vivid images achieved so little. We believed at the time most fiercely in what we were doing. We must have done, for we risked our lives doing it. But in the sum of things I think that we made little difference. Perhaps that was because there was, in all these reports, a missing human dimension. We were outsiders – at best sympathetic observers and at worse no better than war tourists – who stood on the shores of these events and shared the ordeal of the Bosnians only to a very limited degree. That applied to the Serbs and Croats as well as to the Muslims. We had body armour, escape routes, a degree of protection. We even had smokable cigarettes. They did not.

There were things we could sense going on around us but never fully experience or communicate: what it was like to live in a mixed village which went from peace to war overnight, where friends became enemies and neighbours turned into gangs of hostile militiamen, where there was no reliable news but only rumour, where people feared the worst of each other and the fears were self-fulfilling, where village gauleiters and road block Napoleons conducted their reigns of terror and where families of different ethnic origins were torn apart by rediscovered hatreds.

Elvira Simić's story, *The Cry of Bosnia*, provides this missing dimension. Neither I nor any other journalist could have told it. Only she could.

Elvira is a Muslim who married a Serb. She lived in a mainly Serb village near Tuzla. In those times it didn't matter. There were many mixed marriages, just as there were many mixed villages. The old Bosnia was, or seemed to be, a model of ethnic and religious harmony. Its people were encouraged to believe that they were not Muslims, Serbs or Croats. They were Yugoslavs. The Titoist scriptures promote a gospel of brotherhood and unity.

But it didn't last. The dream of the old Yugoslavia and Bosnia which was its central component perished in those terrible days and weeks in the Spring of 1992. *The Cry of Bosnia*, written by Elvira as a diary for her brother in exile, is as vivid an account as we shall ever find of what it was like to be both a witness and a victim at the centre of that storm. It is a story written in tears as much as in ink. It is a story of the triumph of the human spirit and the endurance of the best amid the worst. It is a story that should lead us to question anew why our Governments let this happen.

It is worth remembering also that Elvira herself was one of the more fortunate. She and her son and her husband all survived. Tens of thousands of others did not.

Martin Bell
London, October 1997

PROLOGUE

At the end of 1992 I was going through my second winter in London, running low on my savings.

Bosnia was burning in flames of hatred. Since the spring of 1992 all communications had been cut off.

Here in London very little information filtered through. Often I read in the papers or heard on the news comments like: "Something is happening in Bosnia. We don't know what but will let you know as soon as we receive more information."

The world was expanding its knowledge of geography, having difficulties with spelling names of places darkened by the numbers of dead.

My mother, sister and her husband and their young son were all living in the Tuzla region at the time. My father had died years before, saved from the knowledge that his comrades from the romantic spirit of communist's youth were now at the forefront of the nationalistic parties and had become the creators of this war.

Tuzla was one of two major cities in Bosnia which

became targets for Serbian attacks. The other city was Sarajevo.

In Sarajevo, the Bosnian capital, citizens were dying under the spotlight of the world's curiosity. In Tuzla, citizens were also dying, but away from the gaze of the world.

Susan Sontag was staging a well publicised play in Sarajevo. Her play, *Waiting for Godot*, was tolerated by the world's authorities. Shelling of innocent people in the two cities was also tolerated by the same authorities.

In Tuzla, friends from my theatre days were performing in the trenches to limited audiences. Meanwhile, Bosnia itself had become a huge stage where former Yugoslavia's political leaders and their international colleagues were directing a tragedy. It was a tragedy of gigantic proportions that not just made us cry but hurt its protagonists.

I remember how desperate and helpless I felt one particular night, as I was walking home to my lonely abode in Islington. There was little I could console myself with. Then a clear thought impulse came to me, as I walked along the dark, cold streets of London. *"Life* is what matters. The importance of staying alive and doing something with one's life. Everything else can be taken care of, as long as we *stay alive*."

I recognised this thought impulse. It had first

come to me many years ago when I decided to leave former Yugoslavia. Now it came back to remind me that there is still hope.

Some years before the war started, I was living in various parts of Croatia and Serbia. My university days were over and I had left home to pursue my career.

I saw the communist government fall in 1990 and witnessed first-hand the national euphoria in Croatia.

I also saw the agitators of the Serbian political parties when they started to spread propaganda to strengthen their ranks. I confronted them personally high up in the mountains where I was hiking with friends and witnessed their threatening behavior. This was enough for me to realise that something sinister was brewing under the surface. So I decided to leave.

On crossing the Yugoslav-Hungarian border one evening in July of 1991, my thoughts were not very optimistic. As I gazed back into the disappearing landscape behind me, I was wondering what was going to happen to my country in the next few months. In my wildest dreams, I could not possibly have imagined the terrifying events which were to unfold.

The days of my dearest ones in Bosnia were running out. The thought had been tormenting me for months. I must help them. We must not give up hope.

Although the telephone lines from London to Bosnia were cut off, I discovered there was a way to break into the silence of my country. Radio amateurs and their secret nightly gatherings in the ethers came to the rescue.

This silent army of angels formed a vital link between the world within and the world without.

Sasha from Samobor near the Croatian capital Zagreb became my messenger. I would call him, giving the telephone number of my family and passing on a message. He, in turn, would make radio contact with an unknown friend in Tuzla (perhaps someone I may have known although I never found out the name), passing on my message.

The telephone lines still worked in Tuzla so the messenger would contact my family the next day. The following day I would get a reply via Sasha.

This vital line of communication worked for the next five months. During this time I was desperately trying to organise a safe escape for my family from the hell-hole which used to be my home. It was extremely difficult.

Unknown to me, my sister kept a secret diary. It was her way of crying through ink. It became a necessary expression to relieve the deep pain and sorrow she felt. The diary, together with letters which never reached me, formed an extraordinary document, not unlike Anne Frank's diary. In case she did not survive, they would tell the world about the senseless wastage of human life.

The pages, written from the heart, helped her live in some form of modest dignity as her soul was being consumed by the horrors and madness going on around her.

The plans for my close family did not work out the way I had hoped. We are still separated but *life* is what matters.

My mother, sister and her son managed to escape from Bosnia. They are all alive and well today.

'Everything else can be taken care of.'

Edin Suljic
London, August 1997

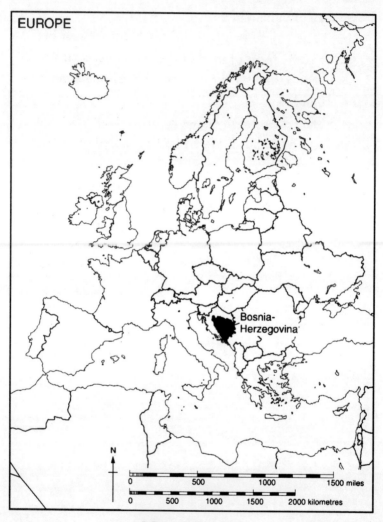

Map of Europe

Map of Bosnia and Herzegovina

1

THE WORLD ABOUT US

APRIL 1992

As I pushed Igor on the swing in the garden this morning, a mixture of fear and happiness spread over his little face. Soft blond tufts of hair danced gaily in the morning breeze. He gazed at me with smiling large blue eyes, filling my heart with the joys of motherhood. He is now 18 months old.

The rising sun reflected its light in the fragile dewdrops on the grass beneath my feet, like tiny crystal balls shimmering with a deep golden glow amongst the pink daisies. The symphony of birds chirping in nearby trees mixed with the sound of flowing water from the stream behind the house.

There was perfect stillness in the mild spring air with a promise of a beautiful day ahead.

Over a year ago we moved here to Jasenica from Sarajevo. Gone are the days of small damp student rooms. Rade was not happy in Sarajevo. Here in these bright rooms overlooking the gentle green hills, rooms which will be filled with Igor's cries and laughter, I thought we would be happy. I was full of hope and optimism, believing in life and love.

Despite the beauty of this spring morning, I suddenly became aware of an eeriness around me. Looking round at the nearby houses and the street outside I saw no-one. The place seemed empty.

For some unknown reason I felt apprehensive. There was a feeling of dejection creeping into my body, as if life had cheated me.

Returning from my mother's house in Tinja yesterday, I found the house of yet another neighbour empty. Her husband had taken her and the children away, probably to Vojvodina.

Anka had been my closest friend since we moved here. We spent most of our time together. Her two young sons used to play with Igor. We went shopping together or on walks in the country with the children picking blackberries. She had helped me adapt to life in Jasenica and also adjust to being a mother. She was a Serb but that meant nothing to me because she was my best friend. Now she was gone without even saying goodbye. What was happening?

Another neighbour had come to say farewell. She was going to Gracanica with her child. By this time I was feeling so despondent.

"Fine, go on and leave me," I thought. "Who cares? In the end I will probably be left here on my own."

Women and children just disappear overnight both here in Jasenica and down in Tinja. The rest of us are left behind with nowhere to go. We keep convincing ourselves there is no panic. Nothing will happen here.

Although there are no signs of danger, I feel more and more insecure. However much I try not to see or listen to what is going on elsewhere, I cannot help but hear the loud talk about arms and night watches to protect our village. There are already control points springing up on nearby roads overnight.

People are becoming more and more distrustful and gloomy. Although we are still living together as a mixed ethnic community, I frequently hear the words "us" and "them" being spoken.

Last night there was awful tumult surrounding the departure of the army units from Tuzla. Nobody knows what is going on. The army had been instructed to vacate the barracks in Skojevska Street and continue moving eastwards towards Serbia. Why all the secrecy?

Most people were seated round their radios yesterday evening listening to the live broadcast of the event. When the column was nearing the outskirts of the city, at Sjenjak, the reporter's voice suddenly became confused, almost panicky, as he excitedly announced that something unforeseen had happened. The column started dispersing, individual vehicles turned back towards the city, and the security people started shooting. Lorries carrying fuel caught fire and there were many dead and wounded. This was repeated this morning on the news and they said the city was now blockaded.

My mind was cast back to the time when I was a young girl. We used to sing a song at school about the army protecting us during our sleep at night. I also remembered the time when young men were called to compulsory military service. Their families were saying sad goodbyes as they left home. Now I am asking "God, what is happening? We seem divided between 'us and them'."

Another children's song came to mind. "If only wars won't happen". The glorious dream of a unified Yugoslavia has been shattered like a child's soap bubble.

Today it seems that the Serbian soldiers protect the sleep of only Serbian children. Croatian soldiers keep vigil over the sleeping Croatian children. But the sleep of my son is only protected by me and my fear, which is huge and dark and has dug its claws into my whole being. Its shadow is cold. It covers the bright blue sky and Igor's laughter. It also casts a foreboding darkness over the days to come.

I was startled from my thoughts of the previous night by the sound of a powerful engine rolling down the street in a cloud of dust. A huge steel giant, thundering like a monster. I quickly grabbed Igor and ran into the house, hiding behind the curtain and trembling. I watched to see what would happen next.

A little later my husband Rade came running into the house, pale and panting. He said this was part of the column which broke up the previous night. Apparently they don't know themselves which way to go. They will probably attempt to take the old road through the forest over Mount Majevica in order to force their way to Serbia. He said anything could happen here and it would be best for me and Igor to hide somewhere for a while.

Along the road outside I could already see family cars loaded with people and their belongings, ready to leave. There were several lorries with old tarpaulin covers hastily stuck with red tape in the shape of a cross, full of women and children. They were all leaving.

At this point I started to panic. I rushed to grab my suitcase from the top of the wardrobe and threw it open in the middle of the room. I quickly filled it with Igor's diapers, clothing, a few toys and some food. The suitcase was too small to take everything I needed.

Meanwhile Rade found a seat for us in a neighbour's car to take us all to Kula in Vojvodina where one of her relations lived.

Only women and children were allowed to leave. The only road which remained open was the old road over Mount Majevica. After Humci it was all Serbian territory. Please God help me!

By this time the telephone lines had been cut off. There was no way I could contact my mother in Tinja. Everything happened so quickly.

My neighbours Gaga, little Boba and Nina watched us depart with wide-open eyes. There was no room for them in any car and they had nowhere to go. They were left behind. Trying to comfort them was hard as I was inconsolable myself. I tried to assure them.

"This is only for a few days. Don't be afraid. All will be well again!"

If only I could believe it myself.

2

JOURNEY INTO THE UNKNOWN

The car was shaking and dragging with its heavy load as it crawled up the steep hill and along the narrow potholed road which was normally used only by goats and a few ox-driven carts carrying wood.

Squashed against each other in the small space, we were frightened and confused.

In the intense heat Igor fell asleep in my lap, red-faced and sweating. What was he making of all this?

We sat in silence, each one left with their own thoughts as we journeyed onwards. We had no idea what would meet us round the next bend or further down the road. How far would we be allowed to travel before being stopped? Would we ever reach our destination? There were many questions and we did not know the answers.

"Where are we going?" I wondered to myself as

the bleak countryside flashed past the car window.

I have never met the people who are going to take us under their roof. Why am I running away? From whom?

People are talking about 'us' and 'them' but for me we are all one. That is until today. Now I realise we are suddenly being forced to declare our ethnic origin. It is like having to slap a sticky label on your forehead for all to see. Someone wants to slot us into categories. It is frightening. Now I don't know where I belong.

Thoughts kept flowing through my mind. "What is really happening? Are we heading for another holocaust, another ethnic cleansing? Surely it cannot happen here? Where was I going anyway? And what about Igor, so young and innocent? What would become of him?"

We were travelling through various settlements: one Muslim, two Serbian, one Croatian, then another Muslim, and so on. They were passing the car window one after another. The last houses in each settlement seemed to join the first houses in the next, almost like holding hands. A never-ending line of human existence that once co-existed in harmony. Now someone was trying to cut the hand that linked them together.

How could the world suddenly change so cruelly? It was surely not the will of the people? Who was behind it all?

In Humci people came into the road to watch our column. Only yesterday they had run from their houses, fearing the Serbs who were coming from Lopare. Yesterday they were friends but today they are distrustful acquaintances and tomorrow they might be enemies bent on exterminating each other. The speed of events is frightening.

In every settlement we passed we were met by sentries, armed people in civilian clothes. Many of them were obviously not used to carrying guns and looked bewildered when they saw the long column of cars loaded with women and children. They just waved us on, not even asking where we were going. The whole scene was unreal, like a bad dream.

After Lopare we were on Serbian territory. The sentries there were already wearing uniforms and looked more professional. They were stopping the cars and asking for identity papers, mostly from the drivers. I was safe. No-one seemed particularly concerned about me. My passport for letting me through was Igor, a young baby firmly asleep on my lap.

Rade's face, darkened by fear and despair as we were leaving, was haunting me. And what about mother? What fear would beset her when she found out that I had left with Igor?

I was trying hard not to think of the beautiful

daisies on our lawn and the winding stream behind the house. Tears were filling my eyes, trickling down my dusty cheeks. In the intense heat and unease of the whole situation, I was sinking into a semi-unconscious state in the back of the car.

The first time I felt real fear was in Bijeljina. A lot of blood was shed there in an ethnic cleansing of Muslims. Some of the houses were damaged. We saw barbed wire along the road, soldiers in uniform, armed, scowling, almost insolent. They were the infamous Arkan's Men (Note 1). A bunker by the roadside aimed machine-guns at us. Fortunately they let us pass.

We were stopped again several more times between Bijeljina and Kula to have our papers checked but now I was no longer afraid. My surname is Serbian because of my husband and no-one can determine my nationality from my first name. This was useful as it did not attract attention to my real roots.

I am a Muslim, one of the persecuted.

Note 1
Arkan's Men is a notorious Serb paramilitary force led by Zeljko Razanjatovic, accused of genocide and humanitarian atrocities.

3

GUEST OR STRANGER?

They were all friendly to me in Kula. Nemanja, our host, is my neighbour's husband's brother. He is married to Jelisaveta, a girl from Kula. They are quite a prosperous family, running their own small restaurant. In addition, Jelisaveta also works for a local firm. Her family owns a butchery.

Although there were eleven of us in the large house, it did not feel crammed. Nemanja and Jelisaveta's son is still in the Yugoslav Army in Banja Luka. The army's top level is now dominated by Serbs, which has contributed to the present tragedy. His garrison is to leave Bosnia soon and they are all very concerned.

I feel lost and a burden to these people. My days are often spent walking aimlessly through the town with Igor. All the streets look very much the same. The trees lining the streets are grey with spray from heavy lorries and traffice passing by. High brick walls are hiding the view into courtyards locked by iron gates behind which chained dogs are barking. Sometimes we pass children absorbed in joyful play. I watch as Igor observes them intently with curiosity. How he would love to join in and throw himself into childlike play.

At the house they avoid all political discussions in my presence but it is sometimes impossible to avoid unpleasant situations. The Serbian television is already mounting an anti-Muslim propaganda.

Yesterday they showed a pile of knives, maces and similar old weapons belonging to museums which were allegedly found in Muslim houses "ready for slaughtering Serbian people." It is the same when we watch the news on television. Nobody is commenting but I feel they keep silent because of me.

I wish I could leave this place and go back home but my feet feel as if they were made of lead. They are stuck in the ground. My pale face blushes with indignation, the palms of my hands become sweaty and my hearts beats hard in my chest. With great effort I stop myself from bursting into tears.

I am longing to hear Rade's voice and the voice of my mother. I am so concerned about what is happening to them. The telephones are not operating. The only news I get is from the painful gatherings around the family's television and radio.

Their son eventually arrived home. There was a lot of excitement yesterday evening when we had a glimpse of him getting off a plane in the current affairs programme on television.

This morning he appeared on the doorstep earlier than anyone expected. They were all overjoyed but I was bewildered. The first thing he did, after greeting all the people in the house, was to fire a whole clip of bullets from his gun outside in the garden. This was followed by a cassette tape playing pro-Chetnik (Note 1) songs. Everybody thought it was great but I was feeling more and more uneasy. How long do I have to stay here?

* * *

Two days after this incident I managed to leave Kula and returned to Bosnia, although I couldn't get back to our village. Radio and television did not report any catastrophic developments in the Tuzla area so I thought I would be safe.

The telephone lines were functioning again. I spoke to mother and she urged me to return home. Rade thought it would be better for me to wait a little longer. I found it hard to make up my mind.

A woman and her daughter, who had also fled here from our village, wanted to return whatever happened. She asked me if I wanted to go back with her. As nobody tried to stop me, I packed my suitcase again. My hosts told me that if things got bad again, I could always return and stay with them. A kind gesture but we both knew it would not be possible.

The sentries looked at us with surprise as we approached the road blocks. Some even attempted to dissuade us from returning. By the time we eventually got back, we found the situation comparatively peaceful. Two days later my two travel companions, the woman and her daughter, suddenly went back to Kula without a word of explanation.

Anyone being a Serb and living in a predominently Muslim area would receive help from Serbs living in other areas. It was safe for my neighbours to leave but not for me. I had nowhere else to go. Not for the moment anyway.

Note 1.
Cetnik. Name of World War II Serbian military forces loyal to the former King of Yugoslavia, Peter II. The Chetniks carried out much of the ethnic cleansing. Their name became synonymous with horror and bloodshed in the eyes of Muslims and Croats. Likewise Ustase were the Croatian forces carrying out killing of Serbs. After World War II, the country fell under the communist rule of Tito. After Tito's death in 1980 and the break-up of the communist bloc in Eastern Europe in the late 1980s, power struggles began, culminating in the Bosnian war.

4

BESIEGED

MAY 1992

The situation is getting worse from day to day. Barricades are going up along the roads. Barbed wire and check points everywhere. We are gradually turning into a war zone.

What remained of the Tuzla garrison, i.e. those who did not go to Serbia, withdrew to Ozren Mountain and took up positions there. You can only enter Tuzla if you have identity papers stating that you are a conscripted worker, but people are afraid to go there anyway. It is rumoured that shells are falling on the city every day.

I saw a man I recognised, an engineer from a local firm, strolling along a street here in Jasenica showing off his beard and Chetnik uniform with an air of pride. Is this a fancy-dress party or a frightening reality?

I leave my house very rarely now. I am getting

anxious. I know all the men are taking turns on watch at the check points but I am against Rade carrying arms.

Where did these guns come from? Are they the same guns which used to protect our country's borders by the army we sang about at school, so that all children could sleep safely? What are they protecting us from now?

"From whom do you want to protect us with these guns?" I asked Rade. My question was serious. "Is it from your neighbour or your school friend with whom you spent years sharing the same desk? And who is going to fire first? Will it be the person with the thinnest nerves or the one who is more fearful of his own life?"

I was becoming more angry.

"Maybe you already know which side you belong to? Do I have to fear you too and be careful what I say to you?"

My heart started to pound in my chest.

"I thought we were safe behind our own walls in this house. I thought we were protected from the madness out there. If you bring a gun into this house, the madness has overstepped its boundary. I don't want to be part of it."

By this time my voice became shaky. My face was hot with perspiration and anxiety.

Rade came towards me. He put his arms around me and gave me a warm hug. He was genuinly trying to calm me but I could feel his own anxiety and worry.

"All right," he tried to assure me, "if you think I am trying to hurt you, it is not my intention ...."

His words escaped me. His voice lacked confidence.

*   *   *

The national parties are having a field day. Everyone wants to wave their little flag or show loyalty to their particular party. No one is sitting on the fence. There is so much national pride. It is quite worrying.

*   *   *

This morning I was woken by nearby gunshots. I jumped out of bed, frightened. Several women were running down the street.

Before dawn the sentries had already noticed that something unusual was happening. Rade hurried out of the house to find out what was going on. I quickly got dressed and started to dress Igor. The suitcase was standing in the corner, still unpacked since my return from Kula.

The shooting did not stop. Rade returned saying

nobody knew what was going on but the whole village seemed to be surrounded. Women and children were advised to take refuge in houses down in the dale which would provide some protection.

Again painful goodbyes, hugs and tears held back. Rade and I gazed into each others' eyes as I hurried away with Igor in my arms. Would we see each other again? How long would it be before we could return? These questions were always burning at the back of our minds.

There were only three houses down in the valley when we arrived. The courtyard quickly filled up with women, children and their luggage. We could hear firing echoing from the village behind. Men with harsh voices hurried us on into the houses and into safety. The rooms were crowded and stuffy. Whispering mothers tried to calm their crying children.

*   *   *

Several days have passed since the shooting began. For two nights nearly a hundred Serbian women and children, two Muslim women and one Croat woman sheltered in the houses down in the dale. There were twenty of us in one room alone. Nobody uttered a single nasty word. We realised we were all trapped in a dangerous situation beyond our control.

With the first faint rays of morning light there was movement and stirring. Children, nervous and hungry, started crying. We had to stay in our rooms and were only allowed visits to the toilets in small groups of two or three. The children became more and more restless as the day wore on.

I managed to gather a small group of about ten children around me and entertained them with storytelling. They were eager to listen.

At daybreak the second day it became clear what was going on. The Muslims from Podorasje, Lisovici and Srebrenik had surrounded Jasenica and Dragunja in order to make the inhabitants give up their arms. The only way out of this place was through Podorasje. All other roads were blocked. The men in the village met to discuss whether they should give up their arms.

On the third day since the siege began I left the sheltered houses to return home. I couldn't endure the chaos any more with all these women and children crammed together. I just had to get out.

On my way home I was surprised to see a bus at the bus station.

"Is it possible to leave Jasenica?" I asked Rade as I got back to our house.

"Yes," he answered, "but all roads are controlled and not everyone can leave."

"I am not going back to these sheltered houses."

Rade could see the anxiety in my face. He did not try to stop me.

The same nightmare repeated itself. I escaped again with Igor, leaving Rade behind, running from one hopeless situation to another.

Rade's face looked hollow and drawn. His eyes were filled with fear and helplessness.

I bordered the bus with Igor, heading for my mother's house.

*   *   *

A few days later a group of unarmed men from the Serb community in Jasenica, carrying a white flag, went to Podorasje to negotiate. They agreed to give up the arms they had received from the Yugoslav People's Army without a fight, although some of them were reluctant.

Five young men in a car set off with their arms. A few kilometres further up the road the car exploded. The road was mined.

Another larger group attempted to cross over to Serbian territory via Majevica but were caught. All the men were taken prisoner. Among them were some people who were genuinely inspired by ideas of a Greater Serbia but there were also some who were confused and were just hangers-on.

People in Tinja were still unaware of the drama which was unfolding only a few kilometres away. Life to them seemed normal.

It was agreed a few days ago to put the arms under joint control. People doubted the Serbs would accept this voluntarily and peacefully. Barricades manned by scowling guards were put up here in Tinja a long time ago. Land mines were scattered around the barricades like terrifying decorations.

Packed suitcases are standing by the front doors. People are waiting.

At night we watch the flashes of artillery fire reflecting from the sky and listen to the distant rumbling of the guns – Brcko, Gradacac, Gracanica .... Are we the next target?

On the eve of the expiry of the deadline for the arms handover we were told it would be best to find shelter somewhere outside Tinja. Rade came to fetch us and took us to our aunt's house in Obodnica. We brought only a few essential belongings. We intended to stay just for a couple of days.

*   *   *

I don't think any more about causes, meanings or reasons. I don't ask questions or weep any more.

My life has become like a boat without oars,

carried by a torrent into the unknown. It is the life of a traveller, a vagabond. I carry all my hopes, fears and all my wealth in one small bundle - inside my heart.

I am no longer capable of making decisions or future plans. Things just happen to me. There is only today, this moment and Igor, a small helpless child in my arms awaking instincts in me to protect his life.

5

A HILLTOP VIEW

JUNE 1992

Obodnica in the gentle evening light seems almost unreal.

The calm air is scented with the fragrance of summer blossoms. Distant sounds of bells can be heard from sheep grazing in the surrounding meadows.

My aunt Hasiba's house is situated high up on a hill overlooking Obodnica. She runs a farm with her husband, two sons and their families.

Behind us are the hills of Mount Majevica, covered in thick forest. On one side we can see the industrial surburbs of Tuzla with their tall dark chimneys. On the other side is Tinja down in the valley, nestling between green meadows, lime trees and silver birches.

The railway line emerges out of the tunnel in nearby Previle and snakes all the way down to the Klisura canyon. There the view of the landscape stops.

Black billowing smoke coming from the direction of the railway station in Tinja spoils the beautiful landscape. It reminds us that a war is going on.

It is not possible to see what is burning. Gentle hills are blocking the view of mother's house. We don't know if it is damaged.

Sitting on the steps of my aunt's house, absorbing the calm evening atmosphere, I felt her strong arm around my shoulders. Memories from my childhood were coming back to me.

"Oh, auntie," I sighed, "if only I could bury my head in your soft pillow with its sweet smell of apples and happy childhood and wake up the next morning free from this terrible nightmare."

She looked at me with deep eyes. A faint smile flickered over her face like a passing candle in the dark. She remembered the carefree moments we had shared when I was a little girl but said nothing.

Things had changed, drastically.

*   *   *

We have no idea what is really happening around us. There seems to be arguments about arms belonging to the Yugoslav Army. The arms were passed on to the Serbs when the army units withdrew from the barracks on Mount Majevica. It was mainly light arms but some heavy armament too. The Serbs objected to having this armament under joint control. That seems to be the reason why Tinja is now in flames.

*   *   *

We are quite comfortable here. There is enough food for us all at the moment but we don't know how long it will last. There are no fresh supplies of food apart from what is produced by the farm. The carefully planned food storage is running out much quicker since the three of us arrived.

Mother and I try to help with household duties as much as we can. Mother does a lot of the cooking but I am not of much use. Apart from kitchen work, I am too inexperienced to work in the garden or in the fields. I don't want to be a burden but there is little here for me to do.

Igor seems very happy here in the midst of all the chaos. There are new faces to excite him, adults, children and animals. He follows everyone around on clumsy legs, offering fistfuls of newly cut grass or wild flowers in his little sweaty hands. When he gets tired in the afternoon, he takes a nap under the shadow of a huge lime tree at the corner of the meadow.

The bliss of innocent childhood! Igor has not

once asked when we are going home or where his father is.

*   *   *

Tonight mother and I were watching the sunset for the seventh time since our arrival here in Obodnica. The column of black smoke is still rising skywards from Tinja. Mother cannot hold back her tears.

It is terrible to sit here helpless, watching these ominous clouds and listening to the sounds of distant artillery fire.

All I can offer mother is a hug. Nothing else can comfort her. There are no words.

We sat close together watching the vast landscape in front of us grow darker.

6

FAMILY TIES

We have been here in Obodnica for over a month. I can't stand it much longer. I want to go home.

Rade has visited several times. He wants to bring Igor and me home to Jasenica. It is the safest place for us, he insists, because nobody happens to be shelling it right now.

Apparently there were only a few casualties in Jasenica during the conflict. About half the male population had been taken prisoner in Tuzla. The residents left behind had established a joint security point into the village. According to Rade, life had now returned to normal. But was it true?

I am keen to go back but every time I bring it up with mother she turns pale like a ghost. The others are trying not to interfere but I can see on their faces that they are afraid for me. They assure us we are not a burden to them and can stay as long as we like.

"As long as there is food and shelter for us, there will be for you too," they insist.

My sweet aunt whispered to me the other day:

"Dear Elvira, marriage is marriage. A husband is a husband and he can take care of himself. But don't forget that you are a mother and have a child to think about. You can see what is happening all around."

She sounded genuinely concerned.

"Neighbours are turning into enemies. Please stay a bit longer with us here. It is much safer."

Inside me everything seems to be falling apart. I want to return to mother's house in Tinja where I can think about everything in peace and come to a decision about my life. I don't feel any real fear. I am convinced that the people there won't do me any harm.

The only thing I am afraid of, if I go back, is looking into the faces of mothers dressed in black, mourning their sons. The blood of their loved ones has been shared amongst them but I was not there to share it with them. I ran away to safety.

It is hard not to feel like a traitor. I am one of many who did not speak up and who did not do anything to try and stop the madness. It got out of control. Now it is too late to stop it.

My greatest fear is that wherever I go, I will hear weeping.

"Oh God, help me out of this goddamn tangled mess." My plea was getting desperate.

*   *   *

They say that Tinja is not safe. It is within range of Serbian artillery from Smoluca. Armed Serbs are believed to be hiding in the caves and forests around Klisura.

We have been told that mother's house is safe. That is all I need to know.

Everything inside me is trembling. The waiting is unbearable. I don't want our relations to witness my personal family drama.

During our stay here we have become very close, my aunt, uncle, cousins, their families and me.

While I was at university I rarely visited them for many years but now I have more than made up for lost time.

I only wish I could let them know how deeply grateful I am that they shared their house with us. Words stick in my throat. Everything is half spoken, yet we seem to understand each other completely. We are all struggling to keep our tears back.

*   *   *

After two months at my aunt's house, we finally said goodbye and returned to Tinja.

I will always remember my aunt whispering:

"Look after yourself and may God be with you."

She was holding me close. I could feel the warmth of her body against mine and the beating of her generous heart. My aunt was like a huge, firm rock as we stood there in the evening twilight. She was strong, yet warm.

I have always loved my aunt. Her closeness made me feel safe. She exuded kindness and unselfishness. Parting from her was hard for me. Her eyes radiated the love of a mother for her child.

We eventually headed back to Tinja, sitting squashed in Rade's car amongst bundles of personal belongings and food parcels.

7

STENCH OF ASHES

AUGUST 1992

Tinja looks spooky. With grieving heart and heavy feet I walk through the place I was born. An ugly blackness is surrounding me, stirring up emotions and anxiety on this warm August day.

Houses are riddled with bullet holes or burnt down. There is a horrible stench of ashes. The station building, shopping centre and surrounding houses have suffered the worst damage.

Scattered along the road are pieces of clothing, pots and pans, children's toys; rags torn out of somebody's life. Through wrecked front doors dark voids are gaping at me.

You can see the odd man here and there walking nervously with a frightened look, quickly taking shelter behind the nearest wall at the slightest sound.

More people than we thought have returned here. Life is quiet, as though hidden under a veil of fear.

We spend most of the time inside the house and rarely venture out. Behind the hills we can hear the rumbling of artillery fire. It is amazing how easily humans become used to these disturbing sounds, like living close to the crashing sound of a giant waterfall. It becomes part of life.

What does stop our breath is the high pitched whistle of rockets as they rip the air. A moment later you hear a deafening detonation.

When this happens we have to throw ourselves on the floor quickly. In the pause between two rockets we then rush half bent over through the cornfields to grandmother's house. One of the rooms has been turned into a shelter with the windows bricked up. The furniture has been pushed against the outer wall. A few blankets and some candles are left on the floor. When it gets quiet again we crawl back to mother's house. This goes on day after day....

The rockets seem to be falling at random with long intervals in between.

"Maybe someone is trying to break the monotony of the long hours spent on duty," I wonder to myself.

"Maybe they are not even aware where the rockets are falling and the destruction they cause?"

A human hand is firing them. Somebody who might have been told that his enemy lives down in the valley. He is told that his enemy wants to take away his house, destroy his place of birth, his religion and his human dignity. So he simply fires, without remorse.

He is not a born killer but this sudden hatred has made him one. Here, from a safe distance, he doesn't see the glazed look of the person he has just killed as he or she was running for their life.

He has been told that if he is not creating fear, he himself would be trembling with fear created by someone else, his enemy. Now he closes his eyes as he pulls the trigger.

While I am lying on the hard floor of our shelter, I keep asking myself again and again:

"Why?"

"Because they hate us." I am told.

"But why?" I ask.

"They have always hated us," they answer.

"It is not true".

Something within me screams out. "Has life in Bosnia been a total lie, until now? Were my friends not my real friends? Was it all just a farce, a sick joke?" I felt angry and confused.

"Is it possible that an entire nation can turn so ugly? Oh no, please God, it cannot be true. Everyone has been cheated," I tried to convince myself.

"Everyone is afraid. They must be or am I continuing to deceive myself?"

I could not possibly give up the dreams and hopes of my youth. My whole future and the future of my son depended on them. In his blood flows half Serbian blood. In him lay the future of this mixed ethnic country, without prejudice or division. He was an integrated part of it, embodying tolerance and peaceful co-existence.

Since my early childhood I have felt any division as a personal insult, a provocation or challenge. Most of my best friends have been Serbs. I chose a Serb as my first love and later I also chose a Serb as my husband.

Now it appears that my path in life has been predestined. I feel trapped in a dark corner, trembling with fear not only for our lives. There is another more horrifying fear. The fear that the belief which has been guiding me throughout my life, namely that *love is stronger than prejudice*, is about to be shattered.

The pinnacle of my belief system is the tiny being of human flesh and blood sitting on my lap. My own son, whose future has at this instant been killed.

"Igor's future, our future and the future of Bosnia can only come into manifestation if this madness stops immediately." I pleaded with God.

"Do something before it is too late, before even more bloodshed and hatred puts its claws too deeply into the human hearts."

But shells are still falling on us like showers from fancy fireworks, except that these are not meant as entertainment.

My heart weighs heavy in my chest. There is no end in sight. The quivering flame of the frail candle will continue to flicker for many more nights in my shelter.

*   *   *

I may never find out what actually happened while we were staying at aunt's house. Information received by word of mouth is always distorted. We don't know what to believe but this is probably what happened.

The first morning after the expiry of the ultimatum, everything was outwardly calm but there was tension in the air. Both sides, Muslims and Serbs, waited behind their barricades for something to happen.

Then a group of armed people dressed in black appeared around the station courtyard at about 11 o'clock. They said the road between the station and the shops was mined. A group of Serbs was dancing and singing in front of the shops under a Serbian flag.

Then there was a phone call to the emergency ambulance service in Srebrenik. Somebody said there was a clash in Podorasje, with many casualties. Three ambulances were under way immediately.

But it was a hoax. When the ambulances arrived in Tinja they were stopped and shot at by Serbs. Two drivers and one male nurse were killed. The rest, three nurses (one wounded) and one doctor managed to escape by crawling along ditches and behind shrubs, out of harm's way.

The initial clash was an act of provocation. It was then established that the Muslims also had a heavy gun, dug in somewhere above Brezje. They started shelling the area round the station.

It was said the Muslims had offered the Serbs another chance to hand over their arms. They also said the road through Upper Tinja in the direction of Tuzla, Dragunja and Jasenica had been open to anyone wishing to go in that direction. I don't know if this was true but I know hundreds of Serbs from Tinja and Potpece left during the night. The majority left for Smoluca as the only "free Serbian settlement" left.

However, Smoluca was surrounded the following day by Muslim forces and remained like a besieged fortress for quite some time. It is impossible to enter Smoluca. The whole area is surrounded by well fortified concrete trenches which were built by the Yugoslav Army some time ago. The Serbs inside Smoluca also have a considerable amount of weapons.

It is believed that people from Smoluca provoked the incident in Tinja. There are some three thousand of them besieged there.

Over the next few days the process of "weeding out" started, i.e. finding those who were hiding in the caves around Klisura and returned to the villages at night, and also searching for people hiding in derelict houses. Many houses were burnt down during this process and the surrounding areas devastated.

Muslim forces from Tinja justified the burning of the houses by saying weapons, ammunition or other suspect material had been found inside. These were probably only acts of hysteria by the people who regarded themselves as "winners".

It was all done haphazardly. Nobody cared about the people who had gone to Smoluca or in other directions and left their houses empty. Some of them may have taken weapons with them while others just left with a few essentials. There may have been weapons left behind for various reasons. Maybe the people did not want to use them. Now they could only watch helplessly from the surrounding hills as flames devoured everything they possessed.

It was later rumoured that most of the fires were started in revenge. Soldiers from burnt-out villages along the river Drina in eastern Bosnia were said to be responsible.

An eye for an eye, a tooth for a tooth, as long as there is something left of the human race. What has become of us?

8

SHELLS AND SHOCKS

They called me from Srebrenik Health Centre. I was asked to report for work. These are war conditions and they are needing volunteers.

I was transferred to the improvised military field hospital in Previle. The ambulance was quartered in one of the large private houses built on a slope on the side of the highway.

I am going to work on foot which is not very safe because of the risk of shelling.

And the work I have to do! I am a dental nurse and now I have to remove dressings from cut-off legs, arms, and blinded eyes. All the victims are so young!

My cousin Ajsa is working in Gradina Hospital in Tuzla and says it is even worse there.

One has to suppress any feelings if one wants to work at all and remain sane.

* * *

Today was a terrible day. The quiet of this beautiful August day was suddenly torn apart by the now familiar whistling sound of shelling.

We ran out of the ambulance to take a closer look. We could follow the trace of the shells clearly. My heart stopped for a second. The shells seemed to fall on the very centre of Tinja. Igor and mother were there.

The shells kept falling one after the other. I could only stand and watch in horror. I leaned against the wall of the house, shut my eyes, covered my ears and counted. Each shell reverberated with a dull thud in every part of my body. Then it stopped. There were nine shells in all.

I waited a few moments, then rushed to the telephone. I could hear the phone ringing in my mother's house and held my breath. Please, please answer!

My mother picked up the phone. She and Igor were safe.

"They were falling very near us but all is well," she managed to say, obviously shocked.

It turned out the shells were falling on the empty spaces around the station. Luckily somebody had aimed badly! I am afraid to go to work tomorrow and leave them all alone.

*　　*　　*

I did not stay long at Previle. Instead I was transferred to the ambulance service in Podorasje. It is a little better here. Only people recovering from lighter wounds are treated, and civilians who need their dressings changed.

I still walk every day from mother's house.

Today here in Podorasje I saw a couple of soldiers lifting a fridge out of a car. I asked where they had got it from.

"From a service store in Tinja," they giggled.

I bit my lip so as not to say anything. I knew perfectly well that what they call 'service stores' are deserted Serbian houses in Tinja.

One house after the other is systematically burgled and emptied of its contents. The best furniture usually ends up in someone's office while the rest is shared amongst petty thieves at night.

My neighbours, who until yesterday were honourable and trustworthy people, are now thieves and criminals.

"What are they dreaming of at night in their stolen beds?" I wondered. "Do they sleep well?"

The fact that our Serbian neighbours had guns hidden in their houses was enough for some Muslims to justify their criminal behaviour.

I know the Serbs were doing the same thing to deserted Muslim houses. Neither the Muslims nor the

Serbs wanted those who had fled their homes ever to return again. They certainly were not expected.

I myself should return to Jasenica with Igor. Rade has been coming here many times trying to persuade me to go back. He has had long discussions with mother and me, trying to convince us that life there is no more risky than it is here.

"Besides," he says, "the ambulance service in Podorasje is much closer to Jasenica than Tinja."

As I looked at Rade's gaunt, pale face, feverish glare and worn clothes, he did not instil much confidence in me. There was no warmth or human compassion in his expression. Yet, Igor was sitting on his lap.

"He is my husband after all," I sighed to myself. "We are a family."

Long before this war broke out, our relationship had started to falter. It was important to me to keep it together. Now, seeing things as they are, I find it hard to admit that our marriage is empty. It has become hopelessly gloomy.

I don't want anyone to say that we split up because he was a Serb and I was a Muslim. I want to stay with him.

*　*　*

I have now gone back home to Jasenica with Igor. Life is so gloomy everywhere. Human faces have become like their abodes, endlessly sad. People are becoming utterly despondent.

We should try and rescue many things before we lose them forever: love, marriage, faith in life, hope for the future.

9

FLOWERS ON THE GRAVE

SEPTEMBER 1992

After almost six months I plucked up some courage and went to Tuzla. Only one bus left in the morning, returning in the afternoon.

It was not easy to board the bus. Every morning there is a long queue of people waiting. Some are on their way to visit wounded relatives in hospital or those imprisoned there. Most of them are women heading for the market to sell some milk and eggs which they can hardly spare from the hungry mouths of their own families. They need to earn a few coins for essential provisions: oil, paraffin, detergents, some flour or a few candles.

Prices of goods are astronomical. Most goods are sold in German Deutschmarks. One kilo of flour costs 1 DM and one litre of oil 2 DM.

Mother's pension, if calculated in German Marks, amounts to 5 DM per month. What I earn is not even enough for a monthly bus fare. That is why I go to work on foot, six or seven kilometres every day. This is possible now but winter is approaching.

I continue to work only because I hope we are going to be paid in goods rather than cash.

The reason for my going to Tuzla is to visit the Academy. It started operating in a small way some time ago but I was not aware of it. Some of the professors are no longer there.

It seems paradoxical that despite all the chaos, people are trying to organise their lives and get back to some kind of normality. They need something to deflect their thoughts from the war and shellings, and focus on life again.

It is now possible to take exams again at the Academy. My exam in child psychology could be ready by the end of September. The two remaining exams could be finished by December. It would give me much personal satisfaction to acquire a degree, even if it will never be used.

Walking through the streets of Tuzla I could see the signs of war. There were broken windows and bullet-ridden facades. Many people were walking around dressed in uniform. Others were crippled by war.

The shops had little to sell. The shelves were almost empty of goods, creating a ghost-like atmosphere. Suddenly I was attracted to a crowd of people queuing up outside a shop. As I got closer I could see the shop was filled almost to the ceiling with goods: sweets, tins of food and fresh fruit. All the prices were in German DM.

It was a scene that only yesterday belonged to the movies. Today it was real, here in Tuzla.

I searched my pockets for loose change and found enough to buy two bananas and a bar of chocolate for Igor and myself.

I visited Vojka, my teacher. She is still there. She looked tired. Her face was marked by deep grief. I wanted to hug her and tell her I understand what she is going through but it is all so difficult.

Vojka has lived almost half her life here in Tuzla. Now, as an old woman, she keeps herself to herself. Although she is not personally to blame for anything, she keeps her opinions quiet to avoid conflict. She is afraid to talk.

I have experienced this myself. More and more often I have to keep my disapproval of things to myself. All the injustices of this cursed war are deeply hurting me. But what can I do?

Tuzla is inundated with refugees. They keep coming every day, crowded onto lorries and buses, or on foot. Behind them they pull miserable bundles and dirty children.

The refugees are roaming aimlessly along the streets until they are shuffled into overcrowded sports halls or empty classrooms. People are sleeping anywhere.

They are offered meagre soups served in large cauldrons. With the soup they receive a slice of bread but not enough to keep the hunger at bay for a whole day. They have to send the children begging from door to door for a handful of sugar, an apple or a cake of soap.

Our aunt Niska has also come to Tuzla as a refugee, with her husband and children. They managed to salvage only what they were able to load on the lorry. The rest, the house, the mill with several tons of flour, the bakery, were all destroyed.

If this madness ceases one day, we will all be homeless paupers.

On the journey back from Tuzla in the bus, I was trying to sort out the many impressions of the day and past memories.

My journey to self-discovery has been very long. For many years I studied stomatology in Sarajevo. During this time I was not happy. I knew it was not a profession for me.

While I was studying, Rade worked in a factory. He found the work both draining and exhausting. His inability to adapt to life in Sarajevo was taking away his zest for life.

Moving to Jasenica, starting a new job and being amongst his own family and friends, would hopefully do him good. I wanted him to be happy. I wanted to see him as the good-spirited and ambitious young man I had fallen in love with.

Despite the move, nothing much changed. His inability to pull himself together and find inspiration, created a strong desire in me to succeed.

I needed to lift myself out of the despair in which we both had found ourselves stuck. Otherwise we would both go under.

It was at this time I started at the Academy in Tuzla. I changed my studies to pedagogy which was more interesting. This time I found myself enjoying what I was learning.

Sadly Rade did not share my enthusiasm. I felt deeply hurt. I made up my mind that with or without him I would succeed. Hopefully my success would stimulate Rade's ambitions. He really wanted to teach literature and do some painting.

Although life here in Jasenica amongst the gentle green hills seemed idyllic, it was not what we were dreaming of a few years ago back in Sarajevo. There was now a war going on around us and a war raging between us.

*　　*　　*

A whole week sometimes goes by without any shelling. Then suddenly something terrible happens.

Shells fell in the middle of a group of people in the market yesterday. There were nine dead. An unborn baby was not sufficiently protected in her mother's womb. She was hit in the head by shrapnel.

A girl was taking flowers to place on the grave of her brother. He lost his life in the war. Now others will have to put flowers on her grave. It is all so sad.

It may sound like a cheap drama being put together like this in my clumsy sentences. But this is real, genuine and painful. Incidents like these occur somewhere every day.

People are dying every day in many parts of this suffering country but three deaths which occurred in the past month struck me hard. One person died of cancer, the other was hit by a shell and the third died from sorrow.

The first one was Rifa, our wet nurse. I saw her this summer for the first time in two years. She had changed dreadfully. From a large woman with rosy cheeks, always smiling, she had turned into a white haired, bony, lethargic old woman. She had no appetite and suffered from stomach pain. A month later cancer was diagnosed. She was operated on twice but it was too late. There were no cytostatics in the hospital. She passed away last month.

Enver, our cousin Shefika's husband, was killed by a shell in a trench near the town of Gradacac. Their daughter told me about a dream about her father after he had died.

The third person was my neighbour from Jasenica. His family left for Serbia at the beginning of the war. He never heard from them again. I saw him walking along the road with his head bowed, like a ghost. Then he shut himself away in his house and never spoke to anyone. They found him lying motionless. He had had a stroke. He died in hospital three days later.

10

FRUGAL TIMES

OCTOBER 1992

There is less and less food around. Times are hard.

Rade has been unemployed for months, ever since the events in Jasenica. Neither am I working any longer.

The improvised ambulance in Previle was shut down. The regular staff returned to their posts and the "newcomers" were pushed out.

I was offered work in Srebrnik but this was not feasible. The money I was offered would not even cover the bus fare, never mind anything else. If I was to spend it on provisions, the money would barely buy a few kilograms of flour. So I gave up the idea. What was the point?

We have to live on charity now. From the local authorities we received a sackful of flour which smelled of fuel and a priest in Dragunja gave us some more flour and a few tins of food.

A neighbour brings me half a litre of milk every day for Igor. I know she hasn't got enough for her own children because she is exchanging milk for flour to make bread. At times someone brings a few beans or a chunk of bacon.

My mother's stock of potatoes is almost exhausted. The crop harvested from her own vegetable garden was very meagre this year. The insects destroyed most of it while we were away. We only managed to mill some maize.

Huge amounts of international aid is sent to Bosnia but the population only receives a small percentage, especially where we live. Most of the supplies disappears in Croatia on its way to Bosnia. A large chunk is stolen by the black market racketeers in their own lorries. They take the supplies to their own store houses and sell it for hard currency. But I have no money left. We are slowly starving.

*   *   *

The long monotonous autumn rain has started. It is getting cold and dark.

It is hard to get out of bed in the mornings. I could easily stay there all day, if it wasn't for Igor. He wakes up early and wants attention. I put him in our bed for a while which calms him down but not for long. I have to get up.

The house is cold in the mornings. There isn't enough coal to keep the stove burning through the night. Although I have to light the stove every morning, I still don't know how to do it properly. The room starts filling with smoke, stinging the eyes and nose, before the draught from the flute sucks it up.

Breakfast is usually an egg or some milk for Igor provided by our kind neighbour. Rade and I have to do with potatoes.

After breakfast we have a long and gloomy day ahead.

Sometimes I stop in front of the mirror. Looking at myself I see a tired and grey face with no make-up. My long dark hair has gone dull. All my clothes are worn out. For over a year I have not bought any new clothing for myself. The skin on my hands is dry and cracked, my knuckles are swollen.

I am only twenty-seven years old but I already feel terribly old and tired.

Rade spends a lot of time away with his parents or with other men from the village. We rarely speak to each other. Without Igor here, the silence would be unbearable.

At night when Rade comes home to bed, I feel myself drawn closer to the wall, away from him. The silence during the cold nights is like an iceberg, separating us. For hours I would lie awake, listening to his breathing. Tears would flow quietly down my face. I could not be bothered to wipe them off.

Everything has been washed away from us. All that remains is raw, naked life.

In the dark of the night I cry out silently: "God help me of out of this hell."

11

DEAREST MOTHER AND SISTER ......

LETTER FROM EDIN *(which never reached Elvira)*

May 1992

Dearest Mother and Sister,

My letters to you are being returned and the telephone lines are mute. Still, I know and feel when you are thinking of me.

I dream about you and I pray for you. Your lives seem unreal, an impossibility, and yet, they are real. Frost grasps my chest and words cease to exist.

I keep repeating to myself that you do exist. You have to exist, despite everything. This absurd human existence, this mind-blowing mercilessness, has to stop. It will stop one day and the moment will come when I can help you.

You are living through intense times. You have to learn quickly in order to survive. I pray that wisdom will enter your hearts in your quiet moments.

There is one word I want to say to you: WAIT. Just wait and be patient. We must wait in order to protect ourselves as the present time only knows of annihilation.

There must be a way out, a solution. Don't give up hope. Be awake and aware of what is going on but remain silent. Just wait. This horror surely cannot continue for much longer.

Take care, my dearest.

Yours, Edin

* * *

LETTER FROM EDIN *(which did reach Elvira)*

October 1992

Dearest Ones,

I have never had such a difficult task and I must not stop to choose the right words. I will try to find those which are clear and which appertain to you.

First – You have to leave distressed Bosnia immediately and escape to me in London. Beasts above you are determined to tear into pieces what remains of Bosnia.

I will do everything to find enough money for your escape. I am sending you some by a British officer who is in the UN forces. He is going to bring it to Tuzla. The rest will be coming via my friends in Zagreb.

I am enclosing instructions on how to obtain transit visas through Croatia.

Secondly – You must not come separately. You must travel together. Leave everything behind you. Put on warm clothing, bring blankets for the cold winter and some little dear personal memento to keep your souls warm. Bring all valuables. You will need them although they may end up in somebody's pocket as a ticket to your freedom. Just be prepared to make these sacrifices. Nothing will ever be the same. All you can truly have is what is in your hearts.

You have to be strong enough to go through all the challenges awaiting you. There is no turning back, no stopping on your way, no saying goodbyes. There is nothing to lose. Winners are those who survive. They are getting a chance to obtain something else in their lives. A human being is neither a home nor a piece of native land. He is neither a country, a nation, nor relations and yet, a human being is part of all of that although in the end we have only ourselves. I know you will understand what I say because of the horror you have witnessed where you live.

I beg you not to live in the illusion that something will change. Whenever someone has survived a cataclysm they will know to build the world in a different way since it is evident that the world which vanished in the cataclysm was no good.

Eternally yours, Edin

*   *   *

LETTER FROM ELVIRA *(which never reached Edin)*

November 1992

Dearest Brother,

Your letter made me feel as if I had been struck by a faint beam of light. Dear God, is it possible that I may escape from this hell?

For a long time I have been dreaming about the journey which would take me far away from this fear, suffering and misery, far away from the innocent and the guilty, from housewives who are skilled in knitting socks and discussing world politics, far away from all those failed schoolboys who have turned into heroes in this fratricidal war. Far, far away where I could forget all this and learn to laugh and rejoice again. But there are still so many steps to climb, so many forms to fill in, so many barbed wires to cross.

But now I have this dream again, and it makes life worth living. There is some hope after all that Igor might grow up somewhere else, far away from the meadows of my childhood where the blossoms have faded into misery and hatred.

Your sister, Elvira

12

LOST FRIENDSHIP

NOVEMBER 1992

It is getting very difficult to visit mother. It is almost impossible to walk with Igor the nine kilometres to Tinja in this cold weather along the snow-covered road.

The buses don't come to Jasenica any longer. To travel to Tuzla or Srebrenik I would have to go on foot to Previle and then take a train. But the train is always so overcrowded.

In addition, the telephone lines to Jasenica are disconnected. We are completely cut off from the rest of the world.

Mother's concern about me living here is so great that I am afraid something might happen to her. I am unable to visit her more frequently. When I manage to get there they all put pressure on me to stay and not return home.

I just don't know where I belong any more. I feel ill at ease both at mother's house and at home, riddled with guilt.

The past events make me feel torn between Serbian and Muslim mothers, crying over their fallen sons. Everyone suffers. The grief is still the same, no matter who you are or what your name is. It makes no difference. We are killing each other but for what?

Who can I talk to? I don't want to worry mother and Igor is too young to understand. And Rade, can he really understand how I feel? He has got his own problems.

We are becoming suspicious of each other. Two human beings living together, yet so far apart. How long can I tolerate this situation? Where is the way out of this tormenting inferno?

"When was the last time I heard laughter?" I suddenly caught myself asking. I have almost forgotten what it sounds like.

If the pathetic situation wasn't so tragic, I would be laughing. It does not seem possible that human beings can sink so low.

I will never understand why Slavoljub from Potpec killed Haznadar from Upper Tinja, or why Muzafer set Dorotej's house on fire. We all went to school together and were friends.

Blessed are those who are far away and will only perceive of this as mere reflections of a distant fire. Will the world ever know what goes on here?

13

IMPOSSIBLE DREAM

DECEMBER 1992

We are waiting and waiting. Our hopes are rising and falling. The transit visas are failing to arrive.

Rade doesn't want us to leave. There is anger and resentfulness in his voice. His conditions for our departure are that the roads must be one hundred percent safe and that we possess all the right documentation. This is absurd and totally impossible.

We hear from time to time that a condition for entering Croatia is a Catholic Birth Certificate. This I will never get, even if I wait a hundred years.

To make matters worse, the Muslims and Croats have started fighting each other in central Bosnia. If war breaks out there, we will be completely cut off here in Jasenica.

* * *

I am trying in every possible way to persuade Rade that Igor and I must leave while we can, even if it is unsafe. But he is deaf as a post. I am not sure whether he is really afraid something might happen to us or whether he is just afraid of being left alone here.

Rade wasn't mentioned in Edin's letter. Maybe that hurt him. Maybe he feels abandoned. He knows that under military rules he cannot leave himself. Is it immense love for us, or immense selfishness?

"Without me," he threatens, "you and Igor cannot go anywhere."

I am begging him to explain why he is against us leaving the country. Although I feel like screaming, I am trying desperately to stay calm. Fear grips me, facing his determination to stop us.

"Nobody will split our family apart," he decides. "If we should leave, then we will leave together."

"But how?" I ask in desperation.

"Across the front line," he replies.

Everyone knows there are dangerous minefields around the front line. He cannot be serious. Behind the minefields on the other side are Serbian troops. It is hard to believe that these hurtful words are coming from my husband. He is not being sincere.

Meanwhile we watch each other like two wounded animals. In this desperate struggle we are devouring the last crumbs of our mutual love.

*   *   *

It was to be our last Christmas and New Year together as a family but I was not to know.

The bleak snow-clad landscape surrounding us looked uninviting. Gone was any glimmer of hope I had managed to hold on to until now.

As there were many ethnic communities in former Yugoslavia, New Year became the central point of festivities. Each community would observe their own traditions as well.

Living in Jasenica around Rade's family I got to know more about the traditional Christmas celebrations.

Memories of my childhood kept my spirit alive. Our smiling faces as children, shrieking with laughter and joy as we chased around the house. The tempting aromas from the busy kitchen and the large dining room table overflowing with delicious fare for the New Year. It was a time for storytelling and getting together with our relations.

How would Igor see his Christmases and New Years as he grew up? What would he remember?

*   *   *

The escape routes are completely cut off. Fighting between Muslims and Croats in central Bosnia is continuing. Despair is filling my whole being.

I have withdrawn into myself. I am no longer arguing with Rade. My tears and anger can do little to change the situation. No argument can help.

"Even if I want to leave, it is too late now," I confessed to Rade.

"Let me go and visit mother instead," I pleaded.

The last few weeks of arguing had tired him out. He could no longer force himself to stop me. In the end he agreed.

"But only for three days," he said.

14

ESCAPE

JANUARY 1993

The night before I would return from mother's house to Jasenica, we heard news on the radio that the roads through central Bosnia were open again. The fighting in Busovaca and Gornji Vakuf had stopped.

My whole body started to shake as if in convulsion. I could hardly wait to hear the rest of the news. The next announcement was that the bus service between Tuzla and Zagreb was operating again. A train would leave Tinja for Tuzla the following morning at 5.30.

"Was I hearing right?" I looked at mother.

"Mum, I am leaving tomorrow. Are you coming with me?"

It was as if a river dam had burst. I was weeping and trembling, unable to hold myself together. Suddenly I had a choice. After months of despair and fighting with my inner self, I was finally free to make a decision which would change all this. A door had opened for me to run away from war, hunger, poverty and my husband. Could this really be a chance to escape?

Only an hour before the departure Alija, our uncle, brought the transit visas. It felt as if an angel from heaven had brought them to me.

This was the hour. It was now or never.

*　　*　　*

My heart was pumping hard. I have left without telling Rade, without his approval and without saying goodbye.

Pain, fear and remorse were tearing through my body but it was too late. The bus was already heading south.

Shells were falling on Tuzla as we left. The echoing sound, as they detonated, followed the bus like a ghostly shadow. We were leaving a nightmare.

Pity those who were left behind.

Everything had fallen into place at the right time, as if some angel was writing the last chapter of our life drama.

"From where did I get the courage to leave, despite Rade's refusal?"

"Who arranged our transit visas?" We had

applied for them soon after Edin's letter back in October and they were brought to us virtually within minutes of our departure.

On the door to my mother's house I left a note for Rade. I asked for forgiveness for the pain I had caused during the last few months. I asked him to try and understand the desperation I had felt which made me leave with Igor. I promised to contact him as soon as we arrived in Zagreb.

Despite our escape, I cannot feel happiness or triumph. There is only endless sadness in my heart.

Our future is uncertain. Life will never be the same again.

The bus crawled across the wounded, devastated country for two days and two nights.

It is hard to imagine what we struggled through. We crossed meadows, drove through forests, along muddy, rutted cart tracks, along the edges of precipices and through burnt down villages.

I shuddered at the sight of these ghostlike sites as we drove past. Literally everything was destroyed in these villages. Not a single house or stable, however small, was spared. Only sooted stone walls jutting up towards the grey sky. No living creature to be seen for miles; not a single sign that life was once thriving here. What had people turned into? What kind of monsters? I shuddered to think.

Towards the end of the second day we were getting closer to the Metkovic border crossing into Croatia. On leaving Bosnia the checking was only formal, but a few yards further on was the beginning of our Golgotha.

We stood in a long queue, holding our papers with shaking hands. I could hear arguments, protests, shrieking. A woman with three small children, a wounded young man with elderly parents but there was no mercy. Whoever did not have a transit visa could not move a step further.

Many had believed the advertisements of the transport companies and left without a visa (Note 1). The journey cost them a fortune they could ill afford. Now they were helplessly pushed back on to the buses to return to Bosnia and Herzegovina. What would be their fate?

I pushed my documents through the window with a trembling hand. It seemed ages before the official's hand stamped it. It could so easily have been refused. It was only a conditional visa.

The official returned the stamped papers and nodded me on.

I staggered more than walked to the bus and fell on to the seat. My whole body pulsated in the rhythm of the four words that I kept repeating: "WE HAVE DONE IT!"

Tears flooded my cheeks as I hugged Igor and mother. We were all crying with relief.

We had lived through a nightmare beyond belief and now it was all over. We were among the lucky ones.

The following morning we were at the bus station in Zagreb. What happened later at the British Consulate and how we eventually ended up in Germany is another story.

Note 1
Well organised underground movements to help Bosnian Muslims escape were golden business. The lucky ones found safe havens somewhere in Europe whilst many did not, despite gambling their last pennies.

EPILOGUE

When the war and ethnic cleansing were at their worst in Bosnia, a famous Bosnian cellist made an appeal to the world's musicians. Vedran Smailovic asked them to bring out their instruments on the stroke of midday on a particular day in July 1992 and play Albinoni's Adagio. Many responded, playing on street corners, in the metro, or in cafes.

This classical piece of music was to become the anthem of Sarajevo's suffering and the haunting image of Mr Smailovic covering his griefstricken face with his hand, head bent down in despair whilst clutching his cello, has since captured the world.

Two years later, I was walking along the South Bank of the River Thames in London. A bronze statue of a cellist playing his instrument, graced the river embankment in the drizzling rain. The chirping of sparrows, children's laughter, the booming of the trains trundling over the railway bridge, sirens of passing boats and the noise from the traffic nearby all merged into a symphony of life. The echo seemed to reverberate through the silent strings of the wet stone figure with his head bent down, captured in his own eternal moment of stillness and oblivious to the richness of life around him.

I often return here to the South Bank. There is something benevolent about a flowing river, an abundance of life that leaves me full of hope. My attraction for surging rivers has always been there, inspiring me and moving me forever onwards to new goals.

As I watched the rain washing over the cellist's immobile face, eyes closed and mouth half open, my thoughts turned to my beloved country. I felt an endless sorrow standing in the midst of teeming life and seeing the large banners with SARAJEVO written on them. Amongst the entertainments offered this evening was a tragedy. "Today - SARAJEVO, the opera." Come and watch!

Sarajevo was now a distant memory of a lively city full of joy and promise which was no longer. Musicians could capture the world and stop it turning for a moment as people were enthralled and enchanted. But they could not stop the horror. No musical chords or lyrics could change the harsh reality. Sarajevo is a tragedy.

What had happened to life in Bosnia? What had happened to the creative artists celebrating life and shaping our future? The opera was telling the story about us. Sarajevo and Bosnia had become symbols of pain but here in London there was no real pain.

The sun suddenly pierced the rainclouds. The colourful flags lining the embankment were swelling in the light breeze, like sails flapping proudly, reflecting the bright sunlight. Flags symbolising freedom, pride and power whilst still being tied with strong ropes to the flagpoles; celebrating life, colour and the movement of the wind, giving true meaning to their existence.

"Yes," I thought to myself, "here is a stage reflecting life and hope. And there is plenty of room on this stage for everyone."

Edin Suljic

Only the Soul has wings to fly

And voice to truly sing ......

Elvira Simić

REFERENCES

Banja Luka. Large town situated in north western Bosnia, known for its beauty. It forms the centre of that region. It had a mixed population before the war but is now a stronghold for Serbs and has become capital of the Serbian Republic.

Bijeljina. Town in north eastern Bosnia on the border to Serbia. Population was ethnically mixed before the war with a majority of Serbs. Many executions of Muslims, Croats and Gypsies took place here by paramilitary forces from Serbia, marking the first major tragedy of the Bosnian war.

Brcko. Large town in northern Bosnia by the river Sava, near border with Croatia. Another place where ethnic cleansing of Muslims took place during the early days of the war. The town is strategically situated for the Serbs, forming a connection between Serb occupied territories in Bosnia and Serbia.

Brezje. Small hamlet next to Upper Tinja.

Busovaca and **Gornji Vakuf.** Two small towns in central Bosnia where heavy fighting between Croats and Muslims took place.

Dragunja. Small Croatian village, neighbouring Jasenica and Podorasje.

Gracanica. Small town 20 miles from Tuzla towards the south west. Mainly Muslim populated.

Gradacac. Small, old town with famous castle bordering on territory occupied by Serbs, mainly populated by Muslims

Herzeg-Bosnia. Before the war Herzegovina was a part of Bosnia and Herzegovina, one of the republics in federal Yugoslavia with a large population of Croats in the west and Serbs in the east. During the war western Herzegovina was proclaimed the Croatian Republic of Herzeg-Bosnia while some eastern provinces were claimed by the Serbs. In both areas Muslims were forced to leave or were ethnically cleansed by brutal murder.

Humci. Muslim village in north eastern Bosnia towards territory occupied by Serbs.

Jasenica. Small village 20 miles from Tuzla and 5 miles from Tinja, mainly Serb poplated.

Kula. Small Serbian town in Vojvodina, close to the north eastern Bosnia.

Lopare. Small town in north eastern Bosnia close to the Serbian border, mainly Serb populated. One of the first places where Muslims were ethnically cleansed.

Metkovic. Picturesque small town in Croatia with mainly Croat population.

Mostar. A beautiful town which was a pre-war symbol of peaceful existence between the ethnic groups. It became a target of Croatian artillery fire.

Obodnica. Large village about 10 miles from Tinja and 10 miles from Tuzla consisting of Lower Obodnica which is Muslim populated and Upper Obodnica which is Croat populated. It has remained in relative peace throughout the Bosnian conflict.

Podorasje and **Lisovici.** Small villages near Jasenica, mainly Muslim populated.

Potpec. Large village near Tinja, mainly Serb populated. It is spread over a large valley, surrounded by hills leading out to the Serbian village of Smoluca on one side.

Previle. Newly built village on flat, rich land next to Tinja towards Tuzla. Mixed Muslim-Croat population.

Sarajevo. Capital of Bosnia.

Smoluca. Large village near Tinja, mainly Serb populated.

Srebrenik. Small, old town with nearby historic castle, about 10 miles from Tinja towards territory occupied by Serbs. Not to be mistaken with Srebrenica.

Tinja. Large village in north eastern Bosnia, 15 miles from Tuzla. Before the war Tinja was ethnically mixed with a majority of Muslims. Upper Tinja is mainly Muslim populated while Lower Tinja has a mixed population.

Tuzla. Second largest city in Bosnia, being a cultural and industrial centre with a university. Population is ethically mixed but with a large majority of Muslims.

Vojvodina. Northern province of former Yugoslavia with independent autonomy until 1990, after which it has been ruled by the Serbian government. Mixed nationalities and ethnic groups live here, mainly Serbs, Croats, Hungarians and Rumainians.

Zagreb. Capital of Croatia.

Note: The publishers regret that it has not been possible to place certain accents over Bosnian place names due to technical difficulties.